274

This book is to be returned on or b
the last date stamped below.

D0513673

THE STORY BEHIND

TIME

Elizabeth Raum

www.heinemannlibrary.co.uk
Visit our website to find out more information about Heinemann Library books.

To order:
☎ Phone +44 (0) 1865 888066
🖷 Fax +44 (0) 1865 314091
🖱 Visit www.heinemannlibrary.co.uk

Heinemann Library is an imprint of Capstone Global Library Limited, a company incorporated in England and Wales having its registered office at 7 Pilgrim Street, London, EC4V 6LB – Registered company number: 6695582

"Heinemann" is a registered trademark of Pearson Education Limited, under licence to Capstone Global Library Limited.

Text © Capstone Global Library Limited 2009
First published in hardback in 2009
The moral rights of the proprietor have been asserted.

Edited by Louise Galpine, Megan Cotugno, and Laura Knowles
Designed by Philippa Jenkins and Artistix
Original illustrations © Capstone Global Library Ltd
Illustrated by Geoff Ward
Picture research by Mica Brancic and Elaine Willis
Originated by Modern Age Repro House Ltd.
Printed in China by CTPS

ISBN 978 0 431114 89 7 (hardback)
13 12 11 10 09
10 9 8 7 6 5 4 3 2 1

British Library Cataloguing in Publication Data
Raum, Elizabeth
The story behind time. – (True stories)
529.7
A full catalogue record for this book is available from the British Library.

Acknowledgements
We would like to thank the following for permission to reproduce photographs: Corbis pp. 4 (© Louie Psihoyos), 14 (© JJamArt), 15 (© Bettmann), 21 (© John Heseltine), 22 (Brand X/© Colin Anderson), 23 (© Reuters) 25–26 (© Bettmann); © DK Images p. 19; Getty Images pp. 6 (Collection Mix: Subjects/Code Red), 7 (Taxi/Bill Losh), 8 (Riser/© B2M Productions), 9 (© Science Faction/Yoav Levy), 10 (© Patricio Robles Gil/Sierra Madre/Minden Pictures), 16 (Stone/© Hugh Sitton), 18 (© Three Lions), 27 (AFP/© John MacDougall); © Mary Evans Picture Library 2008 p. 17; © Photolibrary.com p. 13 (Imagestate RM/Pictor); Shutterstock pp. iii (© stocksnapp), 12 (© Tamara Kulikova); The Bridgeman Art Library p. 24 (© Bildarchiv Steffens).

Cover photograph of the inner works of a watch reproduced with permission of Getty Images (Stockbyte/© John Foxx).

Every effort has been made to contact copyright holders of any material reproduced in this book. Any omissions will be rectified in subsequent printings if notice is given to the publisher.

All the Internet addresses (URLs) given in this book were valid at the time of going to press. However, due to the dynamic nature of the Internet, some addresses may have changed, or sites may have changed or ceased to exist since publication. While the author and Publishers regret any inconvenience this may cause readers, no responsibility for any such changes can be accepted by either the author or the publishers.

Contents

Some words are shown in bold, **like this**.
You can find out what they mean by
looking in the glossary.

The beginning of time

▲ This geologist learns about Earth's past by measuring dinosaur footprints high in the Andes Mountains of Argentina.

Time is a way to measure the past, the present, and the future. We can tell day from night, winter from summer, and young from old. Most people know their exact age. But how do we know the age of Earth itself?

How old is Earth?

Scientists, called **geologists**, have divided Earth's history into time periods called **eras** (see chart opposite). These scientists made their decisions by studying rocks and the fossils (remains) of plants and animals. The earliest era is called the Precambrian Era. This was a long time ago. During almost all of this era there were no plants or animals living on Earth.

13,700 BYA
The "dawn of time" occurs.

4,500 BYA–544 MYA
The Precambrian Era begins and ends.

14,000 BILLION YEARS AGO (BYA)   **4,000** BYA

Geologists believe that the earliest animal and plant life began on Earth during the Paleozoic Era. Fish of various kinds lived in the water. Plants, including large trees, grew on land. The Mesozoic Era was the time of dinosaurs. Crocodiles, birds, snakes, and early **mammals** also lived at that time. It was not until the Cenozoic Era that many of the plants and animals common today began to appear on Earth. Scientists now believe that humans have lived on Earth for about 1.8 million years.

Ideas change ✔

In the 1600s, people believed that Earth was created in 4004 BCE. That would have made it about 5,600 years old at the time. In the 1700s, a French scientist believed that Earth was at least 75,000 years old. Today, geologists study rocks and fossils to learn Earth's age. Scientists now know that Earth is billions of years old.

▼ This chart shows the history of **geologic time**. (BYA means "billion years ago". MYA means "million years ago".)

Era	Characteristics
Dawn of time (13,700 BYA)	The universe is formed.
Precambrian (4,500 BYA–544 MYA)	Earth is formed. There are poisonous gases in the atmosphere (the air surrounding Earth) There is a cold climate (weather conditions) with glaciers (large masses of ice). The first, very simple plants and animals form.
Paleozoic (544–245 MYA)	There are jawless fish, hard-shelled creatures called trilobites, the first land plants, early spiders, and fish with bones. There are the first signs of sharks, **reptiles**, and insects (some with wings). There are cone-bearing trees.
Mesozoic (245–65 MYA)	There are dinosaurs, crocodiles, marine reptiles, turtles, mammals, birds, crabs, frogs, and salamanders.
Cenozoic (65 MYA–today)	Dinosaurs disappear. There is an increase in types of flowering plants, small mammals, trees, first grasses, camels, cats, dogs, horses, and rodents. Homo sapiens (modern humans) appear.

544–245 MYA
The Paleozoic Era begins and ends.

245–65 MYA
The Mesozoic Era begins and ends.

65 MYA
The Cenozoic Era begins. It continues to the present day.

1.8 MYA
Human beings appear.

| 500 MYA | 400 MYA | 300 MYA | 200 MYA | 100 MYA | 0 MYA |

Biological clocks

▲ Some jobs require people to work at night. It is difficult to adjust to a new schedule.

From the beginning of their time on Earth, humans have had special ways of telling time. These built-in clocks are called **biological clocks**. They tell humans when to sleep and when to eat. Scientists have discovered a tiny clump of **cells** in the human brain that tells the body what to do when. These cells help control breathing, temperature, and other things. They tell the heart to beat in a regular rhythm or pattern. The pulse at a person's neck or wrist is a body clock.

Temperature matters

Human body temperature is lowest around 5 o'clock in the morning. As people wake up, their temperature rises. The stomach prepares to digest the food that will soon be eaten at breakfast. Body temperature continues to rise until just after lunch. Then it drops slightly. It rises again until about 7 or 8 o'clock at night.

Scientists continue to study the human brain to learn more about the biological clock. They hope to discover ways to improve health and safety.

A human day ✔

Humans spend about one-third of their lives sleeping. Scientists at Harvard University in Massachusetts, USA, studied people's body temperature. People's body temperature rose and fell over time in a regular pattern. The pattern repeated itself every 24 hours and 11 minutes. Scientists called this pattern a day. This happened no matter when people went to bed or woke up.

▼ Even if people eat well and exercise, they will still grow old.

▲ Children who do not get enough sleep at night may fall asleep in school or be too tired to learn.

Losing sleep

Over half of all adults say they have trouble sleeping at least a few nights a week. Primary school pupils may have problems, too. Some children need a full 10 hours of sleep each night. Others need even more. Lack of sleep makes learning more difficult. It can also cause pupils' behaviour to worsen.

What about you?

Doctors suggest that drinking fizzy drinks with caffeine may cause some children to sleep less. (Caffeine is a chemical that keeps people awake.) Many sleep experts also believe that children who watch too much television may have trouble sleeping. About half of all school-aged children have a television in their bedroom. Is that a good idea? Do you think that drinking fizzy drinks or watching television causes sleep problems for you?

Age	Sleep needs
Newborn babies	16–18 hours a day
Preschool children	10–12 hours a day
School children and teens	9–10 hours a day
Adults	7–8 hours a day

Sleep needs ✔

Getting enough sleep is important for good health. Sleep needs change as a person gets older. Also, some people need less sleep than others.

▼ Scientists who study sleep are performing tests on this young woman. Sensors attached to her head measure her heart rate, eye movements, and brain waves.

Animal clocks

Animals have biological clocks, too. These internal clocks tell animals what to do. They make roosters crow each morning and squirrels gather nuts to store for the winter. Bears know when to hibernate (sleep) for the winter. Scientists have studied jellyfish, worms, starfish, and spiders. They have also studied rats, kangaroos, cats, and many other creatures to learn about biological clocks.

Solar eclipse

A solar eclipse occurs when the moon passes between Earth and the sun. Darkness falls over Earth, making daytime seem like night. Insects fall asleep and birds stop singing. Animals go to their burrows or dens. The eclipse fools their biological clocks into thinking it is night.

Flowers we can count on

Plants also have biological clocks. Each autumn, many trees lose their leaves. In the spring, the weather warms up. Then new leaves grow. In 1751 Swedish scientist Carl Linnaeus pointed out different kinds of flowers. Some change their opening and closing times depending on the weather. Others change their opening and closing times as the length of the day changes. Some, like the morning glory, open and close at the exact same time each day. Other plants, like some bamboo plants, hardly ever flower. When they do, they all flower at the same time across the whole world.

▼ The morning glory opens at exactly 5 o'clock in the morning.

A short history of time

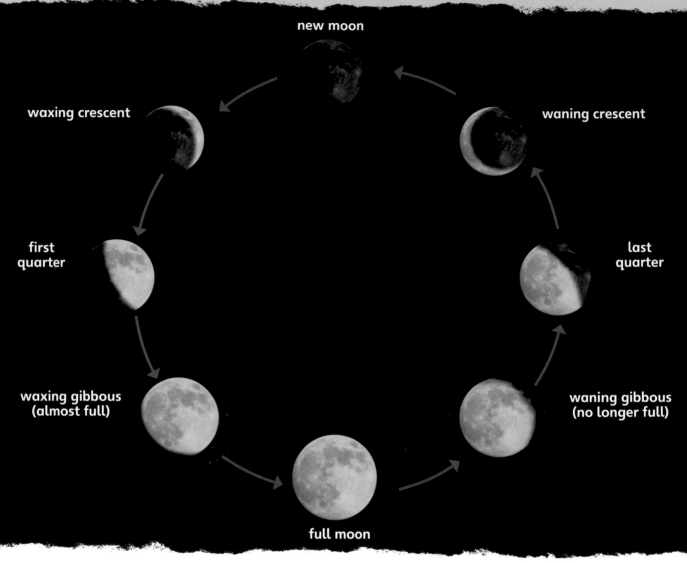

new moon

waxing crescent

waning crescent

first quarter

last quarter

waxing gibbous (almost full)

waning gibbous (no longer full)

full moon

▲ Earth's moon goes through eight different phases as increasing (waxing) or decreasing (waning) amounts of its surface are lit up by the Sun.

It is easy to tell whether it is night or day by looking at the sky. It is much more difficult to know the length of a week or a year. Ancient people noticed that it took the moon about 30 days to go through its **phases** (see diagram). They made **lunar calendars** based on the phases of the moon. Farmers used these calendars to decide when to plant crops.

4241 BCE
The Egyptians use a lunar calendar.

5000 BCE

4000 BCE

Gregorian calendar

Tiny differences may not matter at first. But after 1,500 years, the difference between the sun's year (365.2422 days) and the Roman year (365.25) added up to 10 days. The calendar dates did not match the seasons.

In 1582 CE, Pope Gregory XIII developed the Gregorian calendar. It dropped 10 days off the old solar calendar. This is the calendar used today. Its calendar year is only 0.0003 days longer than the sun's year. People who use the Gregorian calendar will never have to drop days again. Instead, they will skip three leap years every 400 years to keep the calendar on track.

Some places adopted the new calendar right away. Others, like Great Britain and the American colonies, waited until 1752. They had to drop 11 days from their calendars. Japan and China waited even longer to make the change.

▼ Companies often give away free calendars to advertise products. This calendar is from the year 1894.

1582	1752	1873	1949
The Gregorian calendar is created.	The Gregorian calendar is adopted in Great Britain and the American colonies.	The Gregorian calendar is adopted in Japan.	The Gregorian calendar is adopted in China.

1000 1500 2000

Obelisks and sundials

Today, clocks and watches divide time into hours, minutes, and seconds. However, the first clocks measured hours only.

Ancient people noticed that the Sun crossed the sky each day. It made shadows of different lengths on the ground. About 3500 BCE (5,500 years ago), the Egyptians built tall four-sided stone towers to tell time. These towers were called **obelisks**. Later, smaller versions called sundials were used throughout the ancient world. Sundials and obelisks cast a shadow on the ground. People used the length of the shadow to tell the hour. Sundials and obelisks do not work at night.

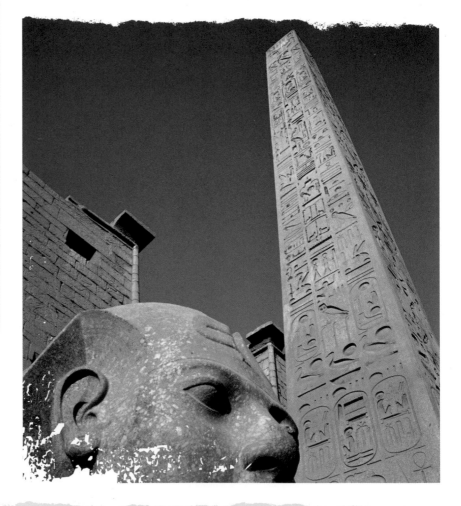

▶ **This Egyptian obelisk used the sun to tell time.**

3500 BCE
Egyptian obelisks help people tell time.

Water clocks

Water clocks told time both day and night. They measured time by how long it took a stream of water to fill a jug. Some water clocks used a series of jars or buckets. Others tipped over, ringing a bell when full.

Water clocks had problems, too. In cold areas, the water froze. In warm areas, it evaporated (turned from a liquid into a gas). People needed a better way to tell time.

 This Chinese water clock was used during the 1300s.

200–1300 CE
The Chinese use water clocks.

0   **1000** CE   **2000**

Tick tock

In about 1285, the first ticking clocks came into use in Italy. These clocks used **gears** to move the hour hand forward. The gears ticked as they moved. These early clocks did not keep exact time. In 1509 German locksmith Peter Henlein used a spring to power clocks. This made smaller clocks possible.

Pendulum clocks

In about 1582, the Italian **astronomer** Galileo developed the idea of the **pendulum**, or swinging weight. He timed the swinging arms of a chandelier (light) hanging from the ceiling. He realized that the time it took to swing from one side to another was always the same. A Dutch astronomer named Christiaan Huygens used this idea to build a pendulum clock in 1656.

▶ Christiaan Huygens built the first pendulum clock in about 1656.

1285
The first ticking clocks are built.

1509
German locksmith Peter Henlein uses springs to power clocks.

1000

1500

In 1761 British inventor John Harrison made a pendulum clock that could keep almost exact time, even on a rolling ship at sea. It also gave sea captains a way to know where they were.

Over time, clocks became smaller and more accurate. By the 1800s, many clocks ran on batteries. Later, they used **alternating current electricity**.

Watch clubs ✔

In the late 1800s, working people in Great Britain and the United States formed watch clubs. Watches were expensive, so each member of the club paid a small amount each week. The club bought one watch with the money. Members drew names to see who got the watch. The club continued until all members owned watches.

▼ **This diagram shows how the swinging pendulum (green and orange arms) turns the gears that move the clock hands forward.**

gears

weight

hour hand

minute hand

pendulum

1656
Dutch astronomer Christiaan Huygens invents the pendulum clock.

1761
British inventor John Harrison invents a ship's clock.

19

2000

World time

During the early 1800s, towns and cities kept their own time. This caused problems when railways began to grow. Passengers had to reset their watches often because each town clock was slightly different.

Standard time

Great Britain was the first country to adopt standard time. By 1852 most British clocks were set to the time in Greenwich, London.

The United States and Canada were too big to use a single time for every town. In 1882 Canadian inventor Sandford Fleming, who worked for the Canadian railway, had an idea. He suggested that the world be divided into 24 equal **time zones**. Each zone would be one hour different from those on either side.

► This map of the world is divided into the 24 equal time zones. The numbers at the top and bottom of the map show how many hours ahead or behind a zone is from the time in Greenwich.

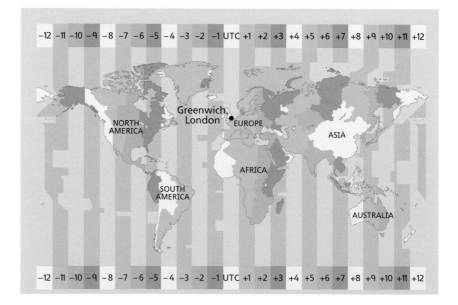

1852
Great Britain adopts standard time.

In 1884 a conference was held in Washington, D.C., USA. People from all over the world attended. They agreed to Fleming's plan. They chose Greenwich as the place where the official (or standard) time begins each day. Today, this worldwide time system is called Coordinated Universal Time (UTC).

International Date Line ✓

The International Date Line is an imaginary line halfway around the world from Greenwich. This is where each new day begins. The date west of the International Date Line is one day later than the date to the east.

▼ This clock in Greenwich shows Coordinated Universal Time.

SHEPHERD PATENTEE
53 LEADENHALL ST. LONDON

GALVANO MAGNETIC CLOCK

This 24-hour clock shows Greenwich Mean Time (GMT)
basis of the International Time Zone System.
British Summer Time (BST) is one hour FAST on GMT
O = Midnight VI = 6am XII = Noon XVIII = 6pm

1882
Canadian inventor Sandford Fleming suggests 24 world time zones.

1884
World time zones are accepted.

1900

Daylight saving time

In 1907 English builder William Willett suggested that Great Britain begin using **daylight saving time** (DST). Moving the clocks forward an hour during the summer would shift daylight hours from morning to evening. At first, most people laughed at the idea. But on 30 April 1916, Germany and Austria did just that. The next October, they returned to standard time. They moved forward again the next summer, and so on. Many other countries did the same.

▼ US inventor and politician Benjamin Franklin first suggested daylight saving time in 1784.

1784
The US inventor and politician Benjamin Franklin suggests daylight saving time.

22

1800

1907
English builder William Willett pushes for DST in Britain.

1900

◀ This clockmaker needs to reset all the clocks in his shop when the time changes.

Britain adopted DST on 21 May 1916. In 1917 Australia and Newfoundland did, too. The United States waited until 1918. Today, about 70 countries use DST. However, countries near the **equator** do not change their clocks. Their days and nights are about the same all year long.

Disagreeing over DST

Many people enjoy the longer summer evenings. Some people believe DST saves energy. Ideally, people will use fewer lights and watch less television in the evening because they will be outside.

On the other hand, some people argue that DST does not add more hours to the day. It shifts daylight hours from morning to evening, so it does not really save energy. Several studies are underway to see whether or not DST saves energy.

Cow time ✔

Cows have a difficult time changing to DST. Some farmers help their cows adjust to DST by changing their milking schedule gradually.

1916
Germany, Austria, Great Britain, and other countries adopt DST.

1917
Australia and Newfoundland adopt DST.

1918
The United States adopts DST.

2000

23

Time travel

▲ These animals were painted on a cave wall in Africa in about 2000 BCE. That is over 4,000 years ago.

In some ways, we are all time travellers. We are born in one time, and with each new day we travel into the future. We can visit the past by going to museums or reading books, diaries, and letters from older periods. Old films, paintings, and drawings also help us see into the past. But how do we go to the future?

Time capsules

Time capsules are a way of telling future people about life today. A time capsule is a container that includes items from the present. It might include voice or music recordings. It might include photos or everyday objects such as dishes, jewellery, pens, or pencils. If you were putting together a time capsule, what would you include?

Visiting the future

Science fiction writers help us to imagine the future. They use science to tell stories about other worlds or other times. Some science fiction writers imagine time machines. But there are no working time machines today.

Time travel is closely connected with space travel. Some scientists believe that by travelling through a black hole (a collapsed star), people will reach the future. Others suggest that a spacecraft could use certain forces in space to pull itself into the past. These are exciting ideas. But for now we will have to use our imaginations to visit other times.

▼ This time capsule is being buried as part of the 1939 World's Fair in New York City, USA.

Atomic clocks

The first **atomic clock** was built in 1948. It used atoms, the tiny parts that make up all things, to tell the exact time. Atomic clocks keep better time than any other clocks. Scientists believe that atomic clocks will lose less than one second every million years. The first atomic clocks were expensive. Today, most people can afford to buy an atomic clock.

Atomic clocks will guide us into the future. Global Positioning Systems (systems that help cars and aeroplanes find their way), the Internet, and space exploration depend on atomic clocks.

▼ This 1959 photo shows US scientist Harold Lyons looking at an atomic clock being built for the US space program.

Time matters

Time has always been important to people. Calendars helped ancient farmers know when to plant crops. Today, clocks and watches help us plan our days. We carry time around with us on our wrists. Whether we are rich or poor, young or old, we all have the same 24 hours each day. How do you use your time? Do you spend it wisely or do you waste it? It is your time to use.

Time words ✔

According to the writers of *The Oxford English Dictionary*, the most commonly used noun in the English language is time. (A noun is a word that refers to a person, place, or thing.) The second most commonly used noun is person, followed by year, way, and day.

▼ The World Time Clock in Berlin, Germany, gives the time in each of the world's 24 **time zones**.

Timeline

(These dates are often approximations.)

13,700 BYA
The "dawn of time" occurs.

4,500 BYA–544 MYA
The Precambrian **Era** begins and ends.

10,000 BYA

3000 BCE
Builders begin creating Stonehenge.

3500 BCE
The Egyptians use **obelisks** to tell the time.

4241 BCE
The Egyptians use a **lunar calendar**.

3000 BCE   4000 BCE

2772 BCE
The Egyptians switch to a **solar calendar**.

753 BCE
The first Roman calendar is used, with a seven-day week.

2000 BCE   1000 BCE

1656
Dutch astronomer Christiaan Huygens invents the pendulum clock.

1582
The Gregorian calendar is created.

1509
German locksmith Peter Henlein uses springs to power clocks.

1600   1500

1752
The Gregorian calendar is adopted in Great Britain and the American colonies.

1700   1750

1907
English builder William Willett pushes for DST in Great Britain.

1884
World time zones are accepted.

1882
Canadian inventor Sandford Fleming suggests 24 world time zones.

1873
The Gregorian calendar is adopted in Japan.

1900

1916
Germany, Austria, Britain, and other countries adopt DST.

1917
Australia and Newfoundland adopt DST.

1918
The United States adopts DST.

1948
The first atomic clock is built and used.

1949
The Gregorian calendar is fully adopted in China.

1950

This symbol shows where there is a change of scale in the timeline, or where a long period of time with no noted events has been left out.

544–245 MYA
The Paleozoic Era begins and ends.

1000 MYA   500 MYA

1.8 MYA
Human beings appear.

65 MYA
The Cenozoic Era begins. It continues to the present day.

245–65 MYA
The Mesozoic Era begins and ends.

1 MYA

46 BCE
The Julian calendar is created.

200–1300 CE
The Chinese use water clocks.

0   1200 CE

1285
The first ticking clocks are built.

1400   1300

1761
British inventor John Harrison invents a clock for use at sea.

1784
US inventor and politician Benjamin Franklin suggests daylight saving time (DST).

1800

1852
Great Britain begins using standard time.

1850

1999
Scientists develop an improved atomic clock.

TODAY
Mobile phones and computers are often used to tell the time.

2000

BYA means "billion years ago".
MYA means "million years ago".

Glossary

alternating current electricity electricity that travels through wires from power stations into people's homes

astronomer scientist who studies the stars and planets. Astronomers study the cycles of the moon and sun.

atomic clock clock that uses atoms, the tiny parts that make up all things. Atomic clocks keep more accurate time than any other clocks.

BCE meaning "before the common era". When this appears after a date, it refers to the time before the Christian religion began. BCE dates are always counted backwards.

biological clock internal cycle or rhythm that tells animals and people when to sleep, eat, wake, and other things

CE meaning "common era". When this appears after a date, it refers to the time after the Christian religion began.

cell small unit that is a basic part of all living things. The human body is made up of billions of cells.

daylight saving time (DST) period when clocks are set ahead to provide more daylight in the evening. Daylight saving time begins in the spring.

equator imaginary line around Earth that is an equal distance from the North and South Poles. At the equator, there are 12 hours of light and 12 hours of darkness.

era period of time. Dinosaurs lived during the Mesozoic Era.

gear wheel with "teeth". In some clocks, gears move the clock hands forward.

geologic time period of time when Earth was forming and developing. Studying geologic time helps scientists understand Earth's past.

geologist scientist who studies Earth's surface. Geologists can work out the age of rocks.

lunar calendar calendar based on the cycles of the moon. The Egyptians used a lunar calendar.

mammal warm-blooded animal that feeds its young with milk and has a backbone and limbs. A dog is a mammal.

obelisk four-sided stone tower used to tell time. The ancient Egyptians built giant obelisks.

pendulum swinging arm. Grandfather clocks have a pendulum.

phase stage in a process. The phases of the moon repeat each month.

reptile cold-blooded animal that breathes air and usually has skin covered with scales or bony plates. Snakes, alligators, and lizards are reptiles.

solar calendar calendar based on the cycles of the sun. Solar calendars are more exact than lunar calendars.

time zone one of 24 divisions of Earth sharing the same time. Each time zone is one hour earlier or later than the one next to it.

Find out more

Books

About Time: A First Look at Time and Clocks, Bruce Koscielniak (Houghton Mifflin, 2004)

Every Minute on Earth: Fun Facts That Happen Every 60 Seconds, Steve Murrie and Matthew Murrie (Scholastic, 2007)

Simple Experiments in Time, Muriel Mandell (Sterling, 2007)

The Time Book: A Brief History from Lunar Calendars to Atomic Clocks, Martin Jenkins (Walker, 2009)

Websites

Explore time at the British Museum.
www.britishmuseum.org/explore/families_and_children/ online_tours/time/time.aspx

Learn more about geologic time.
www.ucmp.berkeley.edu/education/explorations/tours/geotime

Visit the website Clockworks: From Sundials to the Atomic Second.
www.britannica.com/clockworks/main.html

Visit the world clock.
www.timeanddate.com/worldclock

Index